The Way of the Cross
The Way to Life

Stephen J. Binz

Little Rock
SCRIPTURE STUDY

for young Adults

THE LITURGICAL PRESS
ST. JOHN'S ABBEY • COLLEGEVILLE, MINNESOTA

Cover design by Ann Blattner.
Little Rock Scripture Study for Young Adults logo by Don Bruno.
Little Rock Scripture Study logo by Maria Estaun.
Photography: Bob Taylor, cover; Will and Angie Rumpf, page 8, Stephen J. Binz, pages 12, 28, 57 and 70; Marily Nolt, pages 14, 15, 43, 56 and 84; Gail Denham, page 29; Skjold Photographs, page 42; James L. Shalter, page 71; Cleo Freelance Photo, pages 85 and 98.

Nihil obstat: Jerome Kodell, O.S.B., February 3, 1992
Imprimatur: + Andrew J. McDonald, Bishop of Little Rock, February 3, 1992

Scripture quotations are taken from the *New American Bible with Revised New Testament,* copyright © 1986 by the Confraternity of Christian Doctrine, Washington, D.C.

ISBN 0-8146-1698-4

In Memory of
THE MARTYRS OF EL SALVADOR
whose dying and rising has
been a source of life for me

Contents

Introduction to Scripture Study   **9**

Introduction: The Way of the Cross—the Way to Life   **13**

LESSON 1

Day 1 Mark, chapter 14, verses 1-2   **16**
Day 2 Mark, chapter 14, verses 3-21   **18**
Day 3 Mark, chapter 14, verses 22-42   **20**
Day 4 Mark, chapter 14, verses 43-72   **22**
Day 5 Mark, chapter 15, verses 1-32   **24**
Day 6 Mark, chapter 15, verses 33-47   **26**

LESSON 2

Day 1 Matthew, chapter 26, verses 1-16   **30**
Day 2 Matthew, chapter 26, verses 17-46   **32**
Day 3 Matthew chapter 26, verses 47-75   **34**
Day 4 Matthew, chapter 27, verses 1-26   **36**
Day 5 Matthew, chapter 27, verses 27-44   **38**
Day 6 Matthew, chapter 27, verses 45-66   **40**

LESSON 3

Day 1 Luke, chapter 22, verses 1-6   **44**
Day 2 Luke, chapter 22, verses 7-30   **46**
Day 3 Luke, chapter 22, verses 31-71   **48**
Day 4 Luke, chapter 23, verses 1-25   **50**
Day 5 Luke, chapter 23, verses 26-43   **52**
Day 6 Luke, chapter 23, verses 44-56   **54**

LESSON 4

Day 1 John, chapter 18, verses 1-11 **58**
Day 2 John, chapter 18, verses 12-27 **60**
Day 3 John, chapter 18, verses 28-40 **62**
Day 4 John, chapter 19, verses 1-16a **64**
Day 5 John, chapter 19, verses 16b-30 **66**
Day 6 John, chapter 19, verses 31-42 **68**

LESSON 5

Day 1 Mark, chapter 16, verses 1-2 **72**
Day 2 Mark, chapter 16, verses 3-8 **74**
Day 3 Mark, chapter 16, verses 9-20 **76**
Day 4 Matthew, chapter 28, verses 1-10 **78**
Day 5 Matthew, chapter 28, verses 11-15 **80**
Day 6 Matthew, chapter 28, verses 16-20 **82**

LESSON 6

Day 1 Luke, chapter 24, verses 1-12 **86**
Day 2 Luke, chapter 24, verses 13-35 **88**
Day 3 Luke, chapter 24, verses 36-53 **90**
Day 4 John, chapter 20, verses 1-18 **92**
Day 5 John, chapter 20, verses 19-31 **94**
Day 6 John, chapter 21, verses 1-25 **96**

Four Steps of Conversational Prayer **99**

DIOCESE OF LITTLE ROCK
2415 North Tyler Street
P. O. Box 7239, Forest Park Station
LITTLE ROCK, ARKANSAS 72217

Telephone
501-664-0340
FAX 501-664-9186

Office of the Bishop

Dear Friends in Christ:

To know and experience Jesus is the deep desire of every person. In our Catholic tradition, we firmly believe that Jesus is present in His Sacraments and in His Word. It is our tradition to encourage young people to receive the Lord Jesus in the sacraments. In that same tradition, we encourage young people to prayerfully read the Scriptures and discover Jesus present in the Word.

The Little Rock Scripture Program has responded to the hunger for God's Word for many years among adult Catholics. The same dedicated experts have developed this study to respond to those same hungers in young people. I gladly endorse and bless this work, and I encourage you, the young people of our Church, to prayerfully read and study God's Word and to share the fruits of your study with others in your parishes.

I am reminded of the words of Our Holy Father John Paul II to the youth of the world:

> Like all the young people of the world, you are in search of what is important and central in life. . . . You want to put down strong roots and you perceive that religious faith is an important part of the full life that you desire. Permit me to tell you that I understand your problems and your hopes. For this reason, young people, I want to speak to you today about the peace and joy that may be found, not in possessing, but in being. And being is affirmed through knowing a Person and through living according to his teaching. This person is named Jesus Christ, our Lord and Friend. He is the center, the focal point, He who unites everything in love.

I pray that your study of the Scriptures will lead you into a deeper relationship with the person of Jesus Christ. As you open your mind and heart to him, Jesus will lead you to experience the fullness of life that you desire.

Your friend,

✠ Andrew J. McDonald

✠Andrew J. McDonald
Bishop of Little Rock

7

Introduction to Scripture Study

God's word is spoken to us in many ways: through the beauty and wonders of creation, through other people, through quiet prayer, through the voice of our conscience, through the experiences of our lives. Yet God's word has also been spoken in history as God is revealed to people, as God gathers people together and guides them to experience a deeper life full of meaning and hope. Above all, God's word has been spoken in the life, death, and resurrection of Jesus and through the Church, the continuation of Jesus' life through the Holy Spirit.

We are all part of this history of salvation. God's word has been spoken to each of us, and God wants us to respond and enter more deeply into a relationship with God. The Bible is all about God's word, God's communication with people. It is a word spoken centuries ago, yet it is also the word of God spoken today. The same Holy Spirit who inspired the authors of the Bible also inspires each of our lives and leads us to a fuller understanding and more personal response to God, who lives among us and within us.

What an experience it can be to read and study God's word in the Bible! It enhances our understanding of life; it deepens our friendships with others; it gives us hope for the future; it shows us how to know, love, and serve our God.

Purpose of Little Rock Scripture Study for Young Adults

- You will meet and get to know other Christians who are searching for faith just as you are.

- You will be able to talk about your faith with others and share experiences similar to your own.

- You will have the opportunity to grow in your relationship with Jesus Christ.

- You will learn more about the Bible and what it can mean for your life.

• You will have the opportunity of developing a habit of daily Bible reading.

• You will be motivated and supported to live out your faith more visibly.

Materials for the Study

1. *The Bible:* The translations recommended are the *New American Bible, New Jerusalem Bible,* or *Good News Bible* (with Deuterocanonicals/Apocrypha). You should have your own personal Bible. It should be a Bible you can feel free to write in or underline.

2. *Participant's Book:* This book contains the assigned Scripture passages for each day, a commentary on the passages, questions for study and reflection, and space to write responses to the questions.

Your Daily Personal Study

Make a commitment to read the Bible daily. Set aside a particular time that you can be faithful to each day. Find a place where you will be relaxed and free from distractions.

As you begin your Bible study each day, take a moment to say a short prayer. Pray that you will be aware of God's loving presence with you. Ask God to open up your heart and mind so you will truly hear God's voice as you read.

Begin your daily lesson by reading the designated passage. Read it slowly and carefully. As you reflect on the passage ask yourself these four questions: (1) What does the passage say? (2) What does the passage mean? (3) What does the passage mean to me? (4) What am I going to do about it?

Next, read the commentary in this book. It will help you understand the passage better and reflect on its meaning.

The Questions for Each Day

The questions will guide your reflection each day and prepare you for your small-group meeting. Some of the questions can be answered briefly just by paying attention to the Bible (What does the passage say?). Some questions will lead you to a better understanding of Scripture as you reflect on its relationship to its author, the time it was written, and the Church (What does the passage mean?). Some will relate the passage to your life, your relationships, and your faith (What does the passage mean to me?). Some will encourage and challenge you to grow in your faith and put it into action (What am I going to do about it?).

Write your responses to the questions on the lines provided in this book. Writing will help you clarify, organize, and remember your thoughts and feelings.

Your Weekly Small-Group Meeting

Each weekly meeting begins with shared prayer. Then your discussion leader will guide you through the questions for the week. The goal of the small group is not to rush through all the questions but to grow in understanding together. It is an opportunity to learn from one another and to share the joys and challenges of being disciples of Jesus. You will discover that being prepared and being open to your group will strengthen your faith and bring you to a closer relationship with those in your group.

The Wrap-up Time

Following the small-group meeting, all will reassemble. You will spend the remainder of the session sharing together in an activity your coordinator and group leaders have prepared for you. This may be a prayer service, a short talk on the lesson by a speaker, a creative presentation through posters or skits, or a summary of some of the memorable things you have been learning together.

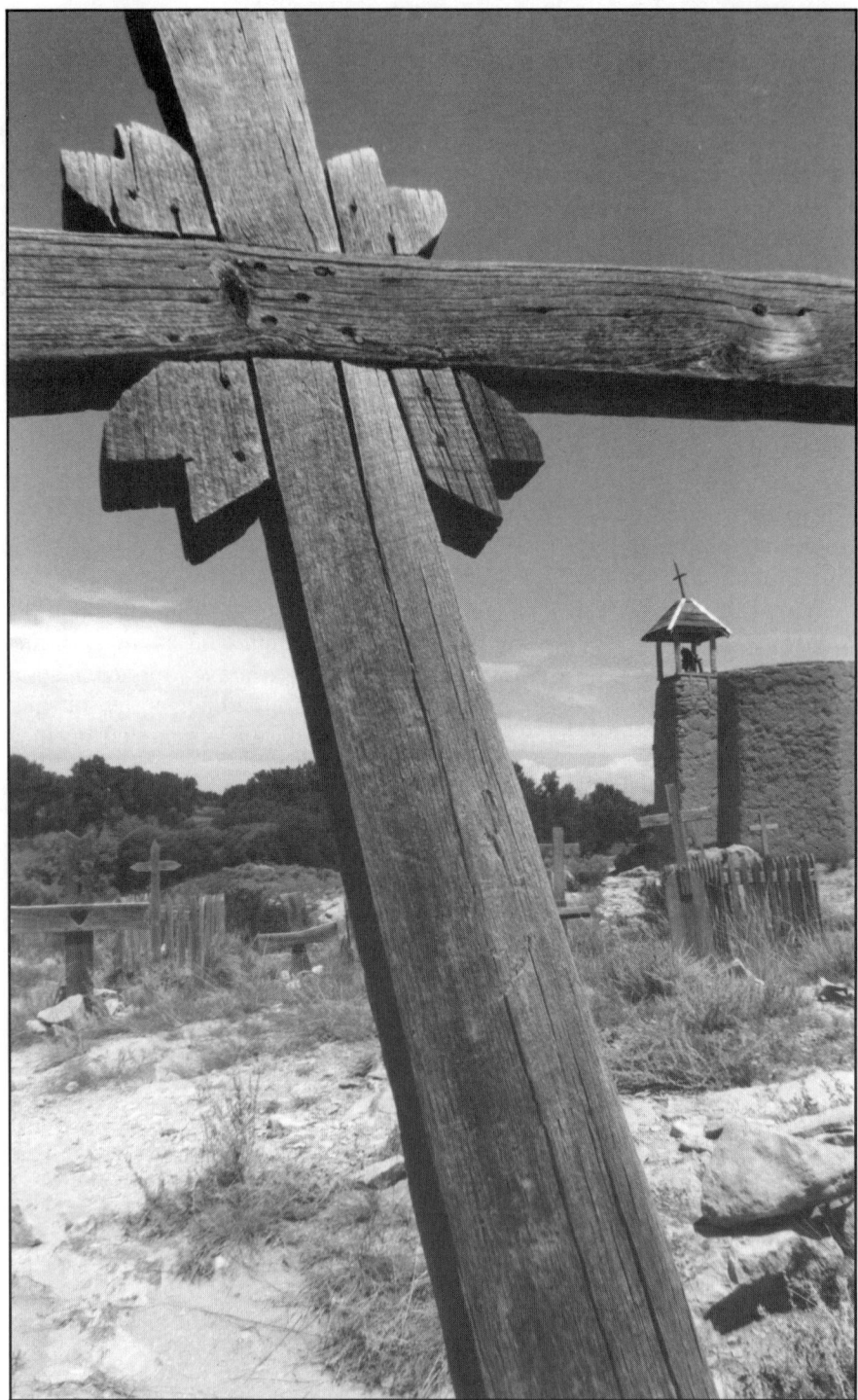

Introduction

The Way of the Cross—the Way to Life

The cross is the world's most common symbol. Seen on mountaintops, on churches, on the walls of our homes, and around our necks, it is a symbol both of the suffering and death of Jesus and of his glorious resurrection. The cross speaks to us of suffering, hardship, and death; it also speaks to us of hope, victory, and life. The cross is the central symbol of our faith in the suffering and risen Christ.

When the disciples of Jesus began to spread the good news of Christianity, the passion, death, and resurrection of Jesus was the core of their message. The Church's earliest proclamation is stated by Paul: "I handed on to you as of first importance what I also received: that Christ died for our sins in accordance with the scriptures; that he was buried; that he was raised on the third day in accordance with the scriptures; that he appeared to Kephas, then to the Twelve" (1 Cor 15:3-5). The early disciples realized that through this event, their Jewish faith, the faith of Israel, had been renewed and fulfilled.

As the early Christian missionaries traveled far and wide, and as the first followers of Jesus began to die, memories of what Jesus said and did were written down. After several decades, four Gospel accounts had been produced proclaiming the life, death, and resurrection of Jesus Christ. Each account differed from the others; each was written in a different time and in a different culture. Each version of the Gospel presents us with a unique portrait of Jesus so that we can know him more fully.

The Gospel accounts are not only about Jesus; they are about us. They are about following Jesus, taking up the cross, sharing his risen life. The word of God is a living word for us. In the passion of Jesus we see the suffering of our own lives and the suffering of the world. Yet, the good news gives meaning and hope to suffering. It shows us that love is refined through suffering; that laying down our lives for others is the way to real life; that death gives way to renewed life.

In the early Christian communities, the saving death and resurrection of Jesus was not just an event recalled from the distant past. It became a living reality as believers gathered to celebrate the Eucharist. Together with them, and with all who have gathered to celebrate the living presence of the risen Lord through the centuries, we proclaim, "Christ has died, Christ is risen, Christ will come again." Particularly in the season of Lent we focus our minds and hearts on the passion of Jesus. Through the Church's liturgy, our private prayer, our self-denial and giving to others, we try to center our lives on the cross. Then on Holy Thursday, Good Friday, Holy Saturday, and Easter Sunday, we celebrate the immense love of Jesus' self-giving for us at the summit of the Christian year.

Each of the Gospel writers found a unique way to respond to the death and resurrection of Jesus. As you open your Bibles to these Gospel accounts, you will be challenged to respond in your own life as well. For each of the first four weeks you will read one of the passion accounts of the Gospels. Then for the final two weeks, you will read the resurrection narratives. As you reflect on the passages for each day, allow the word of God to penetrate your heart as you enter into the heart of Jesus. Discover for yourself that the way of the cross is indeed the way to life.

Lesson 1—The Passion According to Mark (Mark 14–15)
Lesson 2—The Passion According to Matthew (Matt 26–27)
Lesson 3—The Passion According to Luke (Luke 22–23)
Lesson 4—The Passion According to John (John 18–19)
Lesson 5—The Resurrection According to Mark and Matthew (Mark 16, Matt 28)
Lesson 6—The Resurrection According to Luke and John (Luke 24, John 20–21)

Lesson One

Read Mark, chapter 14, verses 1-2

The passion narrative is the summit of Mark's Gospel. All that Mark had been writing about Jesus and his disciples came to its climax in these final chapters. The Cross is the focal point for understanding the meaning of Jesus' life.

There are two fundamental questions at the heart of the Gospel of Mark. The first question is "Who is Jesus?" The second question is "How do I follow him?" Mark's Gospel leads us to the conclusion that we cannot know who Jesus is unless we understand the Cross in his life, and we cannot know how to follow him until we accept the necessity of the Cross in our lives.

Through the passion account we come to understand the meaning of Jesus' life by seeing him as the suffering Messiah. We also realize that the Cross is the test of true discipleship. "Whoever wishes to come after me must deny himself, take up his cross, and follow me" (Mark 8:34). Disciples are those who willingly embrace the Cross, giving their lives for others as Jesus did.

Mark placed the passion account within the context of the Jewish Passover celebration. Each year the Passover commemorated the redemption of the Israelites from slavery to freedom. It began, as all Jewish feasts, at sundown. In the afternoon before the feast, the Passover lamb was sacrificed in the Temple. With the Passover supper that evening, the events of the Exodus were retold and remembered. Only unleavened bread was eaten for supper and for seven days thereafter, remembering the hasty departure from Egypt and the affliction in the desert.

Throughout the Gospel Mark showed the increasing conflict between Jesus and the religious leaders of his day, the chief priests and the scribes. Now they were seeking to arrest Jesus and put him to death. They did not want to arrest Jesus during Israel's feast day because they feared the impact of the crowds. Yet, as the narrative unfolds, we see that they were not in control of events, and Jesus would die on the very day of Israel's Passover from slavery to new life.

Questions:

1. *Why are the passion accounts so central to proclaiming the good news?*

2. *What connections do you see between the events of the Exodus and the passion of Jesus?*

3. *What does the Cross mean in your own life?*

_____

_____

_____

_____

_____

_____

_____

_____

_____

_____

_____

_____

_____

_____

_____

_____

_____

Read Mark, chapter 14, verses 3-21

The tender scene of Jesus' anointing at Bethany is a striking contrast to the scenes of treachery and betrayal which surround it. The woman remained nameless, yet Jesus proclaimed that "wherever the gospel is proclaimed to the whole world, what she has done will be told in memory of her."

The anointing represents the love of a true disciple. In contrast to the other disciples of Jesus, the woman responded in a lavishly generous way. The flask of oil was a rare and expensive ointment. In the Old Testament anointing with oil was a sign of one's dedication to God as a king or priest. It was also a ritual performed on those who were being prepared for burial. The anointing of Jesus was a symbol that Jesus is Israel's royal Messiah and it was also a foreshadowing of his impending death.

Since giving alms to the poor was an important obligation, especially during Passover, this extravagant gesture was challenged by some of the bystanders. They argued that those three hundred denarii could have been given to the poor. Yet Jesus' response, echoing Deuteronomy 15:11, reminded them that even though his own death was near, the disciples would always have the responsibility to care for the poor.

In stark contrast to the selfless generosity of the woman, one of Jesus' closest followers displayed the epitome of selfishness by handing over Jesus for money. The striking difference between the two scenes challenges us to consider our faithfulness as disciples. It is easy to follow Jesus when all is going well, but the true test of our discipleship is in periods of trial and crisis.

Jesus began the Passover meal by emphasizing his close relationship with his betrayer. Notice the progression: "one of you," "one who is eating with me," "one of the Twelve," "one who dips with me into the dish." Jesus' betrayer was an intimate companion. The scene emphasizes that any one of us is capable of betrayal. As the disciples ask Jesus, one by one, "Surely it is not I?" we are pulled into the scene to ask the same question: "Surely it is not I?"

Questions:

4. *What are other examples of generous love shown by true disciples of Jesus?*

5. *How do Psalms 41:10 (9) and 55:13-15 (12-14) express the feelings of Jesus at this moment? When have you felt this way?*

6. *In what ways is your discipleship tested in times of crisis?*

_____

_____

_____

_____

_____

_____

_____

_____

_____

_____

_____

_____

_____

_____

_____

_____

Read Mark, chapter 14, verses 22-42

At the Last Supper Jesus gave new and eternal significance to the ancient Passover meal. Each year Jewish families renew the saving events that made them God's people, rededicating themselves to the covenant. Now Jesus himself was fulfilling all that God had done for the Jewish people throughout history by establishing the new covenant. In his death and resurrection Jesus became for us the new passover. By instituting the Eucharist Jesus gave us the means to share in his saving life and pass over from the slavery of death to the freedom of new life.

Jesus identified the bread of the Passover with his own body, his very self. As Jesus was about to be handed over, broken, and put to death, this ritual action expressed Jesus' gift of himself for others. Jesus identified the cup of wine with his blood, the blood of the covenant. Here Jesus was evoking the covenant ratification (Exod 24:8) when Moses sprinkled the blood of the sacrifice over the altar and on the people. Jesus was saying that his blood, which would be shed at his death, would establish a renewed covenant relationship.

When we share the Eucharist we receive this great gift of Jesus' life. We celebrate the real presence of Jesus with us; we renew the sacrifice of Jesus' death for us; and we deepen our sharing in the new covenant, which joins us to the work of Christ and helps us to work for the coming of his Kingdom.

During these critical hours for Jesus, the disciples were shown at their worst. Peter would deny him, Judas would betray him, and his closest friends could not even stay awake with him as he prayed in the garden. Indeed, as Jesus predicted, none of his chosen disciples would remain with him through his passion and death.

As Jesus experienced emotional agony in the garden, he urged his disciples to "watch and pray." It is this attitude of prayerful readiness and anticipation that we must cultivate in our lives if we are to be faithful disciples of Jesus in times of hardship.

Questions:

7. *How can you enrich your appreciation of the Eucharist (14:22-25)?*

8. *In what ways are you like the disciples of Jesus in the garden (14:32-42)?*

9. *Why did the disciples fail so miserably in the time of crisis?*

_____

_____

_____

_____

_____

_____

_____

_____

_____

_____

_____

_____

_____

_____

_____

Read Mark, chapter 14, verses 43-72

Mark described the total desertion of Jesus' disciples through the starkness of verse 50: "They all left him and fled." Every one of them had good intentions and a real desire to follow Jesus to the end. Yet, they did not understand Jesus' continual teaching about the necessity of the Cross.

In writing his Gospel, Mark was showing the readers of his day the perils of being a disciple. Following in the way of Jesus is risky and difficult. These scenes are a warning to those who enthusiastically follow Jesus in good times, and they are a consolation and hope to those who have failed in their sincere attempts to follow Jesus.

The accusations against Peter spread from a private question by a maid to a confrontation with all the bystanders. Likewise, Peter's denials began as an evasive misunderstanding but developed into a frightened cursing and a sworn rejection of his relationship with Jesus. Peter's overconfidence crumbled when put to the test. The second cockcrow was the dreadful reminder that caused Peter to weep with remorse.

As Jesus stood alone to face his passion, his true identity began to be revealed most fully. Jesus did not want to be proclaimed as the Messiah during his earlier ministry because the people of his time were expecting a glorious liberator who would free Israel from its enemies. It was only when Jesus was seen as the suffering Messiah that his true mission and identity could be understood.

Jesus is the new Temple not made with hands; he is "the Messiah, the son of the Blessed One"; he is "the Son of Man seated at the right hand of the Power." Jesus would not allow himself to be acclaimed in this way during his moments of triumph. Only in his weakest moment, bound as a prisoner, betrayed with a kiss, abandoned by his friends, did Jesus accept these titles unreservedly. At last, in the context of his suffering, these titles can be fully understood. The triumphant power of Jesus is only able to be revealed in the context of his self-giving through the Cross.

Questions:

10. *Why is being a disciple of Jesus a risky undertaking?*

11. *Why was Jesus' identity and mission able to be proclaimed only in his passion (14:61-62)?*

12. *When have you felt like Peter in this scene of failure (14:66-72)?*

Read Mark, chapter 15, verses 1-32

In the scenes of his passion, Jesus was shown to be the royal Messiah and the Suffering Servant, both spoken of by the prophet Isaiah. When asked if he was the King of the Jews, Jesus answered ambiguously. He was not a worldly and political king, but he was truly the expected king in a far deeper sense than they knew. Jesus embodied the figure of Isaiah's Suffering Servant as the innocent victim of violence and hatred: "The Lord laid upon him the guilt of us all. Though he was harshly treated, he submitted and opened not his mouth" (Isa 53:6-7). His mockery and scourging exemplified the harsh treatment of Isaiah's prophecy: "I gave my back to those who beat me. . . . My face I did not shield from buffets and spitting" (Isa 50:6).

The choice between Jesus and Barabbas rested with the crowd, though they were prompted by the chief priests to call for Barabbas. His name literally means "son of the father." The release of Barabbas became a symbol of how God deals with our sins. Jesus takes our sins upon himself so that we might live. We are all sons and daughters of the Father who have been freed and given life by the true Son, Jesus Christ.

The purple cloak and the crown of thorns mocked the claim to kingship. The taunts of the soldiers took up the accusation at the trial which culminated in the inscription on his cross: "The King of the Jews." Irony pervades the scene because what the soldiers did and said was true, but on a level they could not comprehend. Jesus was worthy of their homage, but the true nature of his kingship was hidden in lowly suffering. The inscription on the cross, meant as a humiliation, stated the truth of Jesus' identity. Only here, over the cross, the royal title could be understood in its fullest sense.

In the person of Simon of Cyrene, the Gospel gives us another model of true discipleship. Having come from northern Africa, Simon stepped into the drama of Jesus' passion for a brief moment. Carrying the cross is the way of discipleship. When all the others had abandoned him, the image of Simon with the cross on his shoulders expressed what genuine discipleship is about.

Questions:

13. Why is "The King of the Jews" an ambiguous title for Jesus (15:2, 9, 18, 26)?

14. In what way are you like Barabbas (15:6-15)?

15. Why is Simon of Cyrene remembered in Christian history (15:21)?

_____

_____

_____

_____

_____

_____

_____

_____

_____

_____

_____

_____

_____

_____

_____

_____

_____

_____

Read Mark, chapter 15, verses 33-47

As the early Church celebrated Good Friday, they gathered at the site of Jesus' death and marked the hours of his passion. Mark's Gospel reflects this liturgical remembrance by clearly marking the passion in three periods of three hours each. At the third hour after sunrise (9 a.m.) Jesus was crucified, at the sixth hour (noon) darkness came over the land, and at the ninth hour (3 p.m.) Jesus died.

Jesus' great cry from the cross, preserved by Mark in its original Aramaic, expressed the anguish and abandonment which he felt. The cry is the opening verse of Psalm 22, and we may assume that Jesus continued the psalm as his final prayer. It expresses the desolation of the suffering one, yet ends with confidence in triumph and deliverance.

The death of Jesus is the climax of Mark's Gospel. The moment of death is portrayed with absolute stark brutality as the scene is pierced by the loud scream of Jesus as he died.

The tearing of the Temple veil indicated that the Temple offerings were no longer needed for atonement. The death of Jesus was the final and complete offering for sins. As the veil of the Temple which separated the holy of holies (Exod 26:31-37) was torn from top to bottom, the death of Jesus removed all obstacles which blocked the way of humanity to God.

The death of Jesus opened the way to God for Gentiles as well as Jews. In fact, it was the Gentile centurion who expressed the fullest understanding of who Jesus is: "Truly this man was the Son of God." It was only on the cross that Jesus could be fully understood and his identity proclaimed.

Again true discipleship was expressed in those who were faithful to Jesus. The women, who had followed Jesus throughout his life in Galilee, now followed him to his death. Joseph of Arimathea, who must have been attracted to Jesus during his ministry, now fearlessly requested the body of Jesus and gave him a proper burial in his own tomb. The faithful ones—the centurion, the women,

Joseph of Arimathea—represented what the Christian community would be. Women and men, Gentiles and Jews, together form that community called to share the humble, loving, self-giving life of Jesus.

Questions:

16. *What events show that Mark brought his Gospel to a climax at the death of Jesus (15:33-39)?*

17. *Express in your own words what the death of Jesus means for you.*

18. *What do you see of yourself in the actions of Judas, Peter, the centurion, the women, and Joseph of Arimathea?*

Lesson Two

Read Matthew, chapter 26, verses 1-16

There is great similarity between the Gospel of Mark and the Gospel of Matthew, particularly in their passion accounts. The Gospel of Mark was the chief source for Matthew's work, and in the passion accounts Matthew included every episode from Mark's Gospel. Yet, while the two Gospels appear to be the same, there are many significant differences. Every time Matthew deletes, adds, or rearranges a passage from Mark's account it is done for a specific purpose. The changes in his passion account help to express the unique themes of his version of the Gospel.

Matthew wrote ten to twenty years after Mark in a community composed primarily of Jewish Christians. The Gospel shows that Jesus was firmly embedded in the salvation history of Israel and that he fulfilled God's messianic promises to them. Yet these Jewish Christians had broken away from the Judaism of the Pharisees and were engaged in a passionate conflict with them. While Matthew's Gospel was strongly rooted in the Old Testament Scripture and Jewish tradition, it also showed how the death and resurrection of Jesus foretold the conversion of the Gentiles and the opening of salvation to all peoples.

As the leaders of Israel refused to recognize Jesus and rejected the Messiah, Israel lost its exclusive privilege as God's people. Matthew showed how the Kingdom of God, while not excluding Israel, was broadened to include all the nations. The death and resurrection of Jesus began a new age of salvation, and the promises made by God to Israel were carried on through the Church.

The opening scenes show that the passion narrative is one of strong and shocking contrasts. While Jesus very deliberately informed his disciples about his coming arrest and crucifixion, the secret and confused plotting of Judaism's religious leaders prepared for what was to come. While the woman anointed his body for burial, the disciples argued about the expense. At the same time, Judas sold his master for thirty pieces of silver and set the plot of the antagonists in motion.

Questions:

1. What indicates that Matthew read Mark's Gospel in composing his own?

2. How do the contrasting scenes of the woman and Judas show the dangers of greed for money (27:6-16)?

3. How can selfishness and greed lead people to betray their values and betray other people?

_____

_____

_____

_____

_____

_____

_____

_____

_____

_____

_____

_____

_____

_____

_____

_____

_____

Read Matthew, chapter 26, verses 17-46

For the Jewish culture and nearly every other culture in the world, the meal is a sign of unity, a celebration of family and friendship. The Eucharist, instituted at the Last Supper, became the fullest expression of unity and love for the Christian community.

In this holy feast, Jesus bonds his disciples to himself. It is an eternal bond that Jesus established with his followers, a union that would be perfected as he poured out his life for them. The "blood of the covenant," begun in Exodus and fulfilled in the cross of Jesus, became the bond which unites believers every time the Eucharist is celebrated. This pledge of union represented by the Eucharist made the betrayal of Judas all the more tragic. Judas broke this sacred covenant with Jesus for his own personal gain.

Every time we celebrate the Eucharist we are committing ourselves to this bond of unity with Jesus and with one another. Every time we celebrate the Eucharist, the death and resurrection of Jesus becomes present for us and the effects of that eternal gift become real in our lives.

The death and resurrection of Jesus are our source of life—life with God now and life which lasts forever. The symbols of our Christian faith are living symbols: an empty cross and an empty grave, bread from living seed and wine from living vines, the bread of life and the cup of our salvation. As Jesus looked beyond his death to future glory he said, "I shall not drink this fruit of the vine until the day I drink it with you in the kingdom of my Father." The Eucharist for us is an anticipation of the future and a promise of hope.

Matthew showed that Jesus is a model of prayer for the early Church through his prayer in the garden. Jesus always addressed his prayer to his Father in heaven and prayed that his will be done. Jesus asked his disciples to pray that they may not undergo temptation (literally: "the test"). It was this type of prayer that Jesus had taught his disciples in the "Our Father," and it is this same prayer that we pray together as we join our lives in Christ at Eucharist.

Questions:

4. When and how have you experienced the Eucharist as a bond of unity with God and others?

5. What problems or sufferings have you begged God to remove from your life (26:39)? How might these difficulties fit into God's total will for your life?

6. Pray the "Our Father" as Jesus might have prayed it. What line means the most to you right now? Why?

_____

_____

_____

_____

_____

_____

_____

_____

_____

_____

_____

_____

_____

_____

_____

Read Matthew, chapter 26, verses 47-75

Matthew gave special attention to Judas and Peter in his passion account. They had both become very important in the memory of the Church in which Matthew lived. They served as examples for the way of discipleship—a warning for anyone who would put personal gain above discipleship, and a sign of hope for those who had failed in their discipleship.

It was probably a mixture of motives that prompted Judas' betrayal—ambition, jealousy, greed. Jesus responded, "Friend, do what you have come for." While Jesus knew Judas' intentions, he made it clear that Judas was responsible for his own decision, and like all sinners must bear the consequences of his choice.

The ironic kiss was followed by the violent reaction of another disciple who drew his sword. Jesus used the occasion to reaffirm his stance against violence. Ordering the disciple to put his sword back in his sheath, Jesus proclaimed, "All who take the sword will perish by the sword." By rejecting retaliatory violence Jesus put into practice what he taught in the Sermon on the Mount: "Offer no resistance to one who is evil" (Matt 5:39). "Love your enemies, and pray for those who persecute you" (Matt 5:44).

The questions put to Jesus by Caiaphas at his trial concerned Jesus' identity as "Christ" and "Son of God." Throughout the Gospel, Matthew developed these titles to proclaim the true identity of Jesus. With the title "Christ," Matthew showed Jesus to be Israel's Messiah, foretold by the prophets. "Son of God" made clear the divine authority of Jesus and his unique intimacy with God. Jesus completed the high priest's question by referring to himself as the Son of Man. Alluding to Psalm 110:1 and Daniel 7:13, Jesus referred to his role as judge of the world, his glorious reign, and his return in glory.

The cowardly denial of Peter outside in the courtyard is a strong contrast to the courageous proclamation of Jesus before the high priest. Matthew has emphasized Peter's central role among the disciples as rock of the Church. Now his devastating failure tells us how fragile our own discipleship can be. As the cockcrow pierced the night, Peter began to weep bitterly at his failure and repented.

Questions:

7. *How did Jesus respond to retaliatory violence (26:51-52)? Does Jesus' rejection of violence have implications for discipleship today?*

8. *How and when do you deny knowing Jesus (26:69-75)?*

9. *Why are Judas and Peter so important for Matthew's account of the passion?*

_____

_____

_____

_____

_____

_____

_____

_____

_____

_____

_____

_____

Read Matthew, chapter 27, verses 1-26

Matthew is the only Gospel to narrate the fate of Judas. After seeing Jesus condemned to death, Judas regretted his betrayal and returned the thirty pieces of silver. However, unlike Peter, whose remorse led him to a conversion of heart, Judas despaired and committed suicide.

By describing the last actions taken by both Peter and Judas in the passion narrative, Matthew presented a strong contrast between the two. Peter "went out and began to weep bitterly," while Judas "went off and hanged himself." Judas became the symbol of ultimate loss and betrayal, while Peter was restored, forgiven, and took a prominent role as an exemplary disciple after the resurrection.

Pontius Pilate was the fifth Roman governor of Judea, in charge of the Roman rule in the region from A.D. 26 to 36. Though he lived in Caesarea, he must have spent much time in Jerusalem, especially during the Jewish feasts when it was necessary to control the crowds.

After the religious leaders had determined to put Jesus to death, they brought him to Pilate who could enact the death penalty. Matthew added the scene in which Pilate was sent a message from his wife. Her plea for "that righteous man" further emphasized the tragic conflict between the innocence of Jesus and the envy of the religious leaders. It was the pressure of the chief priest and elders, stirring up the crowds to the brink of riot, that finally forced Pilate's hand to end the trial.

Pilate's dramatic gesture of washing his hands before the crowd while proclaiming his innocence was drawn from the Old Testament. In Deuteronomy 21:7- 9 the handwashing ritual is a plea for repentance and forgiveness: "Absolve, O Lord, your people Israel, whom you have ransomed, and let not the guilt of shedding innocent blood remain in the midst of your people Israel" (see also Isaiah 1:15-16). The gesture dramatizes the fact that everyone had some share in the responsibility for Jesus' crucifixion. It is easy to pass the blame on to others, yet like Shakespeare's Lady Macbeth we cannot cleanse our hands or our hearts with water. True cleansing comes only through the sacrificial love of Jesus poured out for us on the cross.

Questions:

10. *How would you describe the dilemma of Pilate (27:11-26)?*

11. *How do you respond to conflicting pressures from different people? Give examples.*

12. *What can the example of Peter and Judas teach you about your own failures?*

_____

_____

_____

_____

_____

_____

_____

_____

_____

_____

_____

_____

Read Matthew, chapter 27, verses 27-44

The mockery of Jesus as King of the Jews ironically proclaimed his true identity. The scarlet robe, the thorns shaped to resemble a royal diadem, and the reed mockingly imitating a royal scepter became the insignia of Jesus' true nobility. As we see his tormentors kneel before him and proclaim him as king, we know that Jesus is a king in a manner totally different from earthly expectations.

Jesus was mocked and ridiculed throughout his passion. At the house of Caiaphas the servants of the high priest spat in his face and slapped him for his claims to be the Messiah (26:67). After he was sentenced to die the soldiers of Pilate mocked him as King of the Jews. Finally as he hung on the cross in agony he was mocked by three different groups. Those passing by mocked the power he claimed over the Temple. Next, the Jewish leaders ridiculed him as king of Israel. Finally, the two crucified on either side of Jesus reviled him.

The Gospels emphasize the fact that Jesus was tempted to turn away from God's will for his life. Jesus began to experience these temptations at the beginning of his ministry during his forty days in the desert (4:3-9). Each of the temptations—to turn stones into bread, to throw himself down from the Temple, and to worship Satan—had been designed to turn Jesus aside from his mission. Jesus' last temptation—"If you are the Son of God, come down from the cross,"—represented his ultimate challenge. Jesus remained in unyielding obedience and commitment to the mission he received from the Father. Rather than seeking his own glory and his own deliverance, Jesus chose to give himself fully for others.

The final derision of Jesus was an ironic mockery of the very heart of his mission: "He saved others; he cannot save himself" (27:42). In his death on the cross, Jesus enacted his own teaching given during the first prediction of his passion: "Whoever wishes to save his life will lose it, but whoever loses his life for my sake will find it" (16:25). To "save" others was the very meaning of his life, as proclaimed at the beginning of the Gospel: "You are to name him Jesus, because he will save his people from their sins" (1:21).

Questions:

13. *In what ways is it true to say that Jesus was tempted?*

14. *Would Jesus have been "believable" if he had come down from the cross (27:42)? Why or why not?*

15. *How does mockery and ridicule tempt you to turn away from your chosen mission?*

_____

_____

_____

_____

_____

_____

_____

_____

_____

_____

_____

_____

_____

Read Matthew, chapter 27, verses 45-66

Matthew, like the other Gospel writers, deemphasized the physical aspects of Jesus' torturous death. Instead he emphasized the meaning of Jesus' death by showing its fulfillment of the Scriptures. The atmosphere at his death was filled with forboding signs that had been prophesied for the end of the age.

The darkness that came over the whole land expresses the cosmic consequences of Jesus' death and the judgment of God. The prophet Amos had said: "On that day, says the Lord God, I will make the sun set at midday and cover the earth with darkness in broad daylight" (Amos 8:9). Like the ninth plague of Egypt which preceded Israel's deliverance (Exod 10:21), the darkness was a sign of judgment and of hope.

In the Old Testament the quaking of the earth was a signal of God's presence and power being made known. It was a common sign in Jewish literature to show the shaking of the old world and the breaking in of God's Kingdom. The earthquake led to the splitting of the rocks and the liberation of the holy ones from their rock tombs. It alluded to the prophecy of Ezekiel: "Then you shall know that I am the Lord, when I open your graves and have you rise from them" (Ezek 37:13). The resurrection of those who had died before Jesus marked the emergence of the new age begun by the death and resurrection of Jesus.

The final scene of Matthew's passion account shows the Pharisees sealing the tomb of Jesus and posting a guard at the entrance. It reflects the controversy that raged throughout most of Israel during the first century between the Judaism of the Pharisees and those who believed in Jesus. The two groups had radically different explanations of the empty tomb. The unbelievers explained the resurrection as a hoax by charging that the disciples had stolen the body of Jesus from the tomb. Christians proclaimed that the empty tomb was a sign of God's triumphant power in raising Jesus from death. The worst fear of the Pharisees, that the followers of Jesus would proclaim "He has been raised from the dead," became the very core of the Church's faith.

Questions:

16. *Why does Matthew emphasize the darkness and the earthquake rather than the suffering of Jesus at his death?*

17. *Why is Matthew so careful to explain the seal on the stone and the guard at the tomb (27:62-66)?*

18. *In what ways does the death of Jesus bring about a new age for the world and for your own life?*

Lesson Three

Read Luke, chapter 22, verses 1-6

Luke's account of the passion and resurrection of Jesus is the climax of his Gospel and the beginning of the life of the Church. Luke's New Testament writings are really contained in two volumes: the Gospel of Luke and the Acts of the Apostles. The Gospel is the life, death, and resurrection of Jesus and the Acts is the earliest days of the Church after Jesus' death and resurrection.

Luke shows how the qualities of Jesus emphasized in his Gospel become the characteristics of the early Church as it seeks to continue his life and ministry. Jesus' life of prayer becomes the example of prayer characterizing the early community of faith. Jesus' regard for women becomes characteristic of the role of women in the early Church. Jesus' compassion and healing reconciliation become the qualities of ministry in the community of disciples.

Throughout the Gospel, Luke is calling us as readers to identify with Jesus. Especially in his passion account, Luke challenges us to model our life, our attitudes, our service and lifestyle on that of Jesus. Only then can we be the Church that Jesus began, continuing his life in the world today.

Like the other Gospel writers, Luke sets the scene for the passion of Jesus at the time of Passover. Yet, Luke is more explicit in preparing us to see the relationship of Jesus' death and resurrection to the liberation event of ancient Israel. At the Transfiguration of Jesus, Moses and Elijah appeared with Jesus and spoke to him about "his exodus that he was going to accomplish in Jerusalem" (Luke 9:31). The Exodus was the central event of the Old Testament, the founding event of God's people. As God brought them from slavery into a new life of freedom, they were joined to God in the covenant formed in the desert. Jesus' death and resurrection is a new "exodus," establishing the new people of God as they are brought from bondage to a new and abundant life. The Church is the people of the new covenant formed in the saving death and resurrection of Jesus.

Questions:

1. *What is the connection between Luke's two writings, the Gospel and the Acts of the Apostles (Acts 1:1-8)?*

2. *Why were the religious leaders of Israel wanting to put Jesus to death (19:28-48; 22:2)?*

3. *Why is the passion, death, and resurrection of Jesus called his "exodus" (9:31)?*

_____

_____

_____

_____

_____

_____

_____

_____

_____

_____

_____

_____

_____

_____

Read Luke, chapter 22, verses 7-30

Throughout the Gospel of Luke the shared meal is emphasized as the context in which Jesus teaches his disciples the virtues of hospitality, service, humility, and concern for the poor. Here Luke presents the Last Supper as Jesus' farewell meal with his disciples in which he prepared them for his death and for their roles after his departure. Jesus' words to them and the food they shared nourished the disciples for the passion and for their future work.

As Jesus offered the bread and the cup of Eucharist, Luke's account added the words, "which will be given for you" and "which will be shed for you." These words not only predicted Jesus' impending death, but they expressed to his disciples the deepest meaning of his death. It was not simply an act of hatred and violence, not a senseless waste, but it was the central act of Jesus' mission which revealed the meaning of all his other actions.

Jesus' command to "do this in memory of me" helps us to realize that Jesus' actions take us beyond his death to the community of faith after the resurrection. The gathering of the Christian community in Eucharist would link the mission of Jesus and the mission of the Church for all time. The saving life and death of Jesus, his sacrifice for us, would be made present as the bread is broken and the cup is poured out. Yet, it is not just the ritual of Eucharist that the disciples were to continue to do. They were also to make the passion of Jesus the model for the Church's life. Self-giving for others was to become the characteristic of discipleship by which Jesus would continue to live among them.

In his farewell words to the disciples, Jesus reminded them that Eucharist must always lead to service of others. The disciple's concern about their own importance was the opposite of the message of self-giving love proclaimed in the broken bread and the cup poured out. Jesus taught them that Christian leadership is not modeled on the worldly image of power and self-glorification. Jesus' words turned the values of the world upside down. Those who are truly great are those who serve others. Throughout the Gospel Jesus emphasized that those who exalt themselves will be humbled and those who humble themselves will be exalted (14:11; 18:14). Leadership within the Christian community must be modeled on the life-giving service of Jesus which was most fully demonstrated in his death for others.

Questions:

4. *Compare Jesus' farewell discourse to that of Paul in Acts 20:17-38. What parallels do you see?*

5. *How do these verses challenge you to live the Eucharist in your own life?*

6. *In what situations today would Jesus' form of leadership make a positive difference (22:24-27)?*

_____

_____

_____

_____

_____

_____

_____

_____

_____

_____

_____

_____

_____

Read Luke, chapter 22, verses 31-71

Throughout the Gospel, Luke has presented Jesus as a man of prayer. Jesus often prayed alone, away from the crowds, and always prayed before the major decisions of his life. Seeing the prayer of Jesus had prompted the disciples to ask Jesus to teach them to pray. From the beginnings of his ministry at his baptism Jesus had always lived in the will of God through prayer. Now, kneeling in the garden on the Mount of Olives, Jesus prayed fervently and asked his disciples to pray with him. Jesus poured out his heart to the Father and then rose from prayer to face his suffering and death.

Jesus showed his disciples and all of us that prayer must be the foundation of the Christian life. From baptism to death, through a life rooted in prayer we will be assured of God's care even in the darkest moments of life. The example of Jesus shows us that prayer is the source of guidance and strength when we are seeking God's will for our own life or when we are called on to help others in need.

Jesus had been praying for Peter that his faith would not fail in the time of crisis. Jesus knew that the powers of evil would sift his disciples like wheat, causing their faith to be shaken and many to be scattered as chaff is separated from wheat. Though Jesus knew that Peter would fail, he had confidence in Peter and told him, "Once you have turned back, you must strengthen your brothers." Peter insisted that he was ready immediately, without prayer or repentance, to go to prison or even to die for Jesus.

Luke's writings will show us that the prophecies of Jesus concerning Peter did, in fact, occur. Peter was tested and failed (vv. 54-61), he repented (v. 62), and he became a source of strength for others through his leadership after the resurrection (Acts of the Apostles). Indeed, he did go to prison for Jesus. In Acts, he was jailed three times for being a spokesman for Jesus, and ultimately he was put to death as a martyr. The example of Peter shows us that Christian leaders are not those who are exempt from doubts, discouragement, and testing, but those who are supported by prayer and, through repentance and for-giveness, are given the strength and grace to continue.

Questions:

7. *Why was Peter unable to be faithful to Jesus in the moment of crisis (22:31-34, 54-62)?*

8. *How can the example of Jesus' prayer strengthen your own life of prayer (22:39-46)?*

9. *In what situations do you need to pray, "Not my will but yours be done" (22:42)?*

_____

_____

_____

_____

_____

_____

_____

_____

_____

_____

_____

_____

Read Luke, chapter 23, verses 1-25

In Jesus' trial before Pilate and Herod, Luke demonstrates that Jesus was innocent and that the proceedings against him were unjust. In the opening verses the religious leaders brought four charges against Jesus. We see that each of these charges has two levels of meaning: on the historical level they are clearly false charges, yet on a deeper level there is a profound truth in each of them that summarizes the mission of Jesus.

In the first charge, the leaders accused Jesus of "misleading our people." Certainly the prophetic teachings of Jesus did not corrupt the people, yet we realize that the words and actions of Jesus were meant to bring about a radical change of direction for God's people. The second charge, that "he opposes the payment of taxes to Caesar," is clearly false on the surface since Jesus had taught just the opposite when challenged in the Temple. Yet, ironically there is a deep truth in the charge since Jesus' teaching to pay "to God what belongs to God" (20:25) challenged the sovereignty of Caesar with a higher authority. The third charge, that he claims "he is the Messiah, a king," also has two levels of meaning. That Jesus is a political king challenging Roman authority is obviously a false charge. Yet clearly throughout the Gospel Jesus is portrayed as God's anointed king, the royal Davidic Messiah. The final accusation, that "he is inciting the people with his teaching," as a charge of political sedition is false, yet certainly all of Jesus' teaching was intended to stir up people.

Jesus had been hauled by his captors from the Mount of Olives to the house of the high priest (22:54), then to the council chamber of the Sanhedrin (22:66), then to Pilate (23:1), to Herod (23:7), then back to Pilate (23:11). With Jesus declared innocent three times by Pilate (vv. 14, 15, 22), Luke's account stresses that Jesus is not a guilty criminal but a victim of injustice. As such, Jesus was an example to his followers who would also be unjustly persecuted. Jesus had warned them: "They will seize and persecute you, they will hand you over to the synagogues and to prisons, and they will have you led before kings and governors because of my name" (21:12). The Acts of the Apostles shows how the treatment of Jesus was carried on in the unjust persecution of the Church.

Questions:

10. *In what ways do people still act like Pilate today (23:1-15)?*

11. *What do you think Herod asked Jesus (23:9)? Why would Jesus not answer him?*

12. *How do you decide whether to accept persecution or fight back?*

_____

_____

_____

_____

_____

_____

_____

_____

_____

_____

_____

_____

_____

_____

Read Luke, chapter 23, verses 26-43

Those who accompanied Jesus to his crucifixion formed a motley congregation. Simon of Cyrene carried the cross of Jesus. The women of Jerusalem, who "mourned and lamented him," were a welcome contrast to the condemning crowds who demanded Jesus' death. As Jesus had wept over Jerusalem, Jesus told the women to weep for their city and their children as he predicted Jerusalem's punishment and destruction. The two criminals who also accompanied Jesus on the way to the cross are mentioned only in Luke's account. All throughout his life Jesus had a special bond with the sinners and outcasts of society. Now Jesus would walk with these companions to his death.

At his crucifixion, after suffering such pain and humiliation, Jesus expresses forgiveness for those responsible for his death. Jesus' words, "Father, forgive them, they know not what they do," is totally consistent with the whole life of Jesus. He had taught his disciples to forgive others (17:3) and to love their enemies (6:35); now Jesus was expressing his teaching in the fullest way by forgiving his executioners.

The two criminals who had accompanied Jesus on the way to the cross and had been crucified on each side of him now embody two very different responses to Jesus. One criminal continued the mocking of Jesus, challenging his identity as Messiah and Savior: "Are you not the Messiah? Save yourself and us" (v. 39).

The other criminal is a model of repentance. He openly confessed his sin (v. 41) and turned to Jesus for help (v. 42). As a result of his repentance, Jesus promised him a place in paradise with him that very day. The criminal's trust in Jesus and his willingness to repent had brought him salvation.

The contrast between the two criminals on the right and left of Jesus is dramatic. They represent the two conflicting judgments that people will continue to have about Jesus. Some, like the first criminal, maintain a skeptical stance waiting for some evidence that Jesus is truly who people claim him to be. Others, like the second criminal, realize they are lost without God and put their trust in the power of Christ to save them. That repentant criminal represents all of us and the saving effects of Jesus' death for us.

Questions:

13. *What can you learn from Jesus' forgiveness of those responsible for his death (23:34), (Acts 7:60)?*

14. *In what way is the response of the second criminal a summary of the Gospel message (23:40-43)?*

15. *Among those who accompanied Jesus to his death, who do you identify with the most? Why?*

_____

_____

_____

_____

_____

_____

_____

_____

_____

_____

_____

_____

Read Luke, chapter 23, verses 44-56

The death of Jesus is reported by Luke in six quick verses. He shows the two cosmic signs preceding his death, the death itself, and the reactions of the people who were present. It is significantly different from Mark's account as Luke changed, added, or deleted many verses from his source.

The darkness in Luke is a symbol of the powers of evil at work. Jesus had said at his arrest, "This is your hour, the time for the power of darkness" (22:53). It is this darkness that will be scattered by his death and resurrection. The tearing of the Temple veil, before the death of Jesus in Luke, symbolizes the way to God now open for all people. The two signs speak of the effects of Jesus' death upon the whole earth and on all people.

Luke shows that Jesus died in a spirit of serene trust in God's will. Instead of reporting Jesus' cry of abandonment in the words of Psalm 22 as in Mark's Gospel, Luke says that Jesus died with the peaceful words of Psalm 31 on his lips: "Into your hands I commend my spirit." Though the powers of darkness seemed triumphant, Jesus died with confident trust in a faithful God.

Three sets of witnesses responded to Jesus' death. The centurion, witnessing what had happened, "glorified God"—the response of one who recognizes the saving presence of God. He was the first in a long line to give public witness to the meaning of Jesus' death. Next, "all the people who had gathered" reacted to Jesus' death by "beating their breasts"—a gesture of repentance by one seeking God's mercy after recognizing sinfulness.

The third set of witnesses were "all his acquaintances" and "the women who had followed him from Galilee." These women had followed Jesus during his mission in Galilee (8:1-3), had come with him to Judea, had remained with him to his death, and finally stayed until his burial in the tomb.

These faithful women were the last to leave the stage of Luke's passion narrative. Yet they left only to prepare for their return. They did not give up on Jesus, but returned to minister to him even in death. Their witness is the clearest model of faithful discipleship in the Gospel. Because of their steadfast devotion they would be the first witnesses to the resurrection of Jesus.

Questions:

16. *What is the meaning of the darkness and the torn veil of the Temple at the death of Jesus (23:44-45)?*

17. *Why would Luke use Psalm 31 as Jesus' final prayer on the cross?*

18. *Why does Luke emphasize the loyalty of the women (23:49, 55-56)?*

_____

_____

_____

_____

_____

_____

_____

_____

_____

_____

_____

_____

_____

Lesson Four

Read John, chapter 18, verses 1-11

The central truth of the Gospel of John is that Jesus is the Word of God who has come into the world to reveal God's overwhelming love for us. The whole Gospel is a gradual revelation of the glory of God's only Son. From his pre-existence with the Father "in the beginning," he comes to reveal the Father and then to return to the Father.

The passion is the summit of the Gospel and the fullest expression of God's love for the world. After a series of "signs" throughout the Gospel that revealed his glory, the death of Jesus became the final and most effective sign. There is no more convincing sign of love than to give one's life out of love for others.

In John's Gospel the cross of Jesus is both a sign of death and a sign of victory. Jesus referred to his death as a "lifting up" (3:14; 8:28; 12:28) which implies both the crucifixion in which Jesus is "lifted up" on the cross and his exaltation in glory. When he is lifted up from the earth on the cross, Jesus reveals himself most fully and communicates the life of God to those who accept him and commit themselves to him.

This blend of death and triumph is present throughout John's passion account. The opening scene plunges us into the darkness of the night, the violence of arrest, the horror of betrayal, the threat of armed soldiers, and the danger of pending execution. Yet these gruesome realities do not obscure the triumphant glory of God's Son. Jesus is not a helpless victim, he is one who gives his life freely as an act of love for the world. His glory luminates these dark scenes and confronts the powers of darkness.

Jesus identified himself to the arresting party with the words "I AM." John makes known the power of this identity as he notes that they "turned away and fell to the ground." "I AM" is the mysterious name of God revealed to Moses in Exodus 3:14. The reaction of Judas and the captors of Jesus as they cringe and fall down is the typical reaction throughout the Bible when the presence of God is manifested. Jesus' confidence and his divine authority dominate the scene as he begins the tribulation toward which his whole life had led him.

Questions:

1. *Look up other "I AM" statements (4:26; 6:20; 8:24, 28, 58; 13:19). What is the deeper meaning of this self-identification of Jesus?*

2. *Why is John 15:13 a summary of John's passion account?*

3. *How is the Cross both a sign of death and a sign of victory for you?*

Read John, chapter 18, verses 12-27

In the other Gospels Jesus had remained almost silent before his accusers. He had played the role of the Suffering Servant, silently absorbing the violence of his persecutors. In John, Jesus speaks boldly and openly challenges his opponents. He is the light of the world, speaking the truth in the face of falsehood, and challenging the forces of darkness. Just as Jesus had always "spoken publicly to the world" (18:20), he continues to fearlessly speak the truth.

Peter's denial of Jesus is woven together with the interrogation before Annas. While Jesus boldly proclaimed his identity and mission before the high priest, Peter floundered and wavered in fear and weakness. Peter's denial, "I am not" (18:17, 25), is a strong contrast to Jesus' bold "I AM" in the garden. Peter chose to deny his identity and his discipleship.

John is unique in introducing "another disciple" into the account of Peter's denial. This unnamed disciple is referred to several times throughout John's narrative and is also called "the other disciple" and "the one whom Jesus loved." He appears at critical scenes in the passion and resurrection accounts: the Last Supper, the denial of Jesus, the crucifixion, the empty tomb, and the resurrection appearances. In each of these scenes the other disciple is shown in contrast to Peter. This unnamed disciple is shown as a model disciple and seems to have been a particularly important figure for the community of John.

John contrasts light and darkness, truth and falsity, and portrays the struggle of discipleship as Peter wavers between them. Peter had been called by Jesus into the light, yet in the moment of threat and crisis, he fell back into darkness. Peter's urgent determination to follow Jesus even to death (13:37), had been met with Jesus' understanding and confidence: "You cannot follow me now, though you will follow later" (13:36). The darkness of Peter's denial will be scattered by the light of Jesus' resurrection, and Peter will become the great proclaimer and witness of the early Church.

Questions:

4. *Why does Peter respond so differently in 13:37 and in 18:17?*

5. *When have you felt like Peter in this scene?*

6. *How is the passion account also about Christian discipleship?*

_____

_____

_____

_____

_____

_____

_____

_____

_____

_____

_____

_____

_____

_____

_____

_____

Read John, chapter 18, verses 28-40

The center of John's passion account is the trial before Pilate. The trial is dramatically heightened as many of the themes developed throughout the Gospel are brought to a climax here. It is ultimately about the choice that all of us must make: the choice to acknowledge the truth or to be consumed by falsehood.

Throughout the trial John shifts the scene back and forth from outside the praetorium where the Jews are gathered to the inside where Jesus is held. Pilate moves from the frenzy of the outside to the eloquent defense of Jesus within. This dramatic technique expresses the struggle taking place within Pilate as he weighs his own conviction of Jesus' innocence against the pressure from without to condemn him.

John's Gospel alone gives the reason for the trial before Pilate: only the Romans had the right to put anyone to death. When Pilate wanted the Jews to judge Jesus by their own laws and deal with him accordingly, the Jews reminded him that they did not have the right to execute anyone. John sees this as a fulfillment of God's plan that Jesus be "lifted up" on the cross.

Jesus' identity as king is the central issue of the trial. The interrogation and responses are filled with irony and double-meanings. To be a "king" is the very purpose of Jesus' mission in the world. Yet, Jesus says, "My kingdom does not belong to this world." His is not a dominion within the world of darkness and deceit; rather, he reigns in the world of light and truth. His sovereignty is expressed not through worldly power, but through witnessing to the truth.

Jesus is the truth (14:6); to know him is to know God. Those who are open to the truth are able to recognize Jesus as the genuine revealer of God and accept his saving message. Those who cling to falsehood cannot recognize the truth and reject him. Pilate's famous question, "What is truth?" is one which we all must answer. When we live in the light and listen with our heart, we will know the truth.

Questions:

7. Why do the Jewish authorities bring Jesus to Pilate (18:30-31)?

8. What do you think Pilate meant by his question in verse 38?

9. Why is truth so often difficult to recognize (18:37-38)?

_____

_____

_____

_____

_____

_____

_____

_____

_____

_____

_____

_____

_____

_____

_____

_____

_____

Read John, chapter 19, verses 1-16a

The central theme of the trial before Pilate, the kingship of Jesus, is displayed here with dramatic irony. The major symbols of royal power are mockingly conferred on him. He is given a crown, but it is a crown of thorns. He is given a purple cloak and proclaimed as king, but their tribute is marked by beatings rather than acts of homage. The sarcastic cry, "Hail, King of the Jews!" is really proclaiming the deepest truth. Through the seeming powerlessness of Jesus, the divine source of all genuine authority is revealed.

Pilate continued to move back and forth from outside to inside. Inside he was influenced by the serene eloquence of Jesus; outside he was pressured by the outcry of the crowd. Pilate's confusion and reluctance to take a stand is dramatized as he oscillated back and forth. The scene is really about what is taking place inside Pilate. He is like a pendulum swinging—from truth to falsehood, from responsibility to indifference, from decision to apathy.

Pilate tried to placate the crowd by punishing Jesus and presenting him to the crowd as a harmless pretender. He displayed Jesus as an unfortunate and broken man who should not be taken seriously. In response the same crowd who had cried out, "Hosanna . . . the king of Israel," just a few days earlier, now hailed their king with the shout, "Crucify him!"

The final words of the chief priests, "We have no king but Caesar," proclaim a dreadful judgment upon themselves. Israel had always claimed God alone as its true king. God's kingship was made visible in the anointed king of the House of David, and it was expected that the future Messiah would come to establish God's reign on earth. Now the priests of the Temple were rejecting their messianic king and proclaiming their allegiance to the worldly powers of the emperor Tiberius.

In John's Gospel the crucifixion of Jesus takes place on Preparation Day, the day before the feast of Passover. Jesus was handed over to be crucified at the very hour the Passover lambs began to be ritually slaughtered in the Temple.

64

While thousands of lambs were being killed in preparation for the great feast of Jewish liberation, the Lamb of God who takes away the sin of the world (1:29) was offered up on the cross.

Questions:

10. *Why does John put the mockery of Jesus at the climactic point of his trial scene (19:1-3)?*

11. *Why does John place Jesus' death on the Preparation Day for Passover (1:29; 19:14)?*

12. *Give other examples of how genuine authority is shown in humility and seeming defeat.*

_____

_____

_____

_____

_____

_____

_____

_____

_____

_____

_____

_____

Read John, chapter 19, verses 16b-30

John's Gospel uniquely shows that the death of Jesus on the cross is the fulfillment of all that Jesus came to do. The Old Testament was completed and a new age of salvation began. The death of Jesus was not an end; it was the beginning of a new people and a new covenant. It was the founding event of the Church.

As Jesus is crucified he is proclaimed as king to all the world. His throne is the cross. His retinue are the criminals crucified on both sides. The royal proclamation, "Jesus the Nazorean, the King of the Jews," is written in the three languages to proclaim his kingship to the whole world. The "I.N.R.I" above the cross in Christian art is an abbreviation of this title in Latin: "Iesus Nazarenus Rex Iudaeorum."

Even the garments of Jesus become highly symbolic in John's Gospel. They were divided into four parts, representing the four directions of the earth to which the Church will spread. Yet the tunic remained undivided, symbolizing the unity of the Church. That unity was a continual theme throughout the Gospel and the focus of Jesus' final prayer at the Last Supper (17:21-23). Universal and united are the characteristics of the Church which Jesus established in his death.

The birth of that Church is symbolized at the foot of the cross. Jesus' words to his mother and his beloved disciple, "Behold, your son . . . Behold, your mother," form a new spiritual family. It is the final work of Jesus; as he dies the Church is born. All who experience the salvation that comes through the cross of Jesus become part of that new family which is the Church.

John tells us that Jesus was "aware that everything was now finished." All that Jesus had come to do was about to be completed. His words, "I thirst," express his desire to fulfill his Father's will. He is to "drink the cup" which the Father gave him to drink. Only after Jesus drinks the cup of suffering and death can he become the source of living water for all others who thirst (7:37-38). At his death he becomes the source of life for all.

Questions:

13. *Why is the inscription over the cross written in three languages (19:20)?*

14. *How does John show that the death of Jesus is the birth of the Church?*

15. *What is your favorite image of Jesus on the cross?*

_____

_____

_____

_____

_____

_____

_____

_____

_____

_____

_____

_____

_____

_____

_____

_____

_____

Read John, chapter 19, verses 31-42

The decision not to break the legs of Jesus and the piercing of the side of Jesus are both unique to John's Gospel. Though John was obviously writing about events that actually happened, he was also expressing in each event something about the deeper meaning of Jesus' death for us.

John carefully notes that the legs of the other two bodies were broken while Jesus' legs were not. The legs were broken to hasten their death because the Sabbath was drawing near and the bodies were to be taken down from the crosses. However, since Jesus was already dead, they did not break his legs.

The Scripture John quotes, "Not a bone of it will be broken," is a paraphrase of several Old Testament passages describing the lamb of the Passover. The lamb was to be sacrificed without mutilation and then eaten whole. Added to the fact that Jesus was crucified at the same time as the Passover lambs were being sacrificed in the Temple, this is a further indication that Jesus is truly the "Lamb of God who takes away the sin of the world" (1:29).

When the side of Jesus was pierced with a lance, immediately blood and water flowed out. The thrust of the lance demonstrated for the witnesses that Jesus was truly dead. Yet, John's reason for featuring it was to demonstrate that from his death there flows new life for all who follow him. When the passover lamb was slaughtered, the priests of the Temple were to catch the blood in basins of silver and gold as it poured from the sacrificial victim. The blood, understood as the very life of the victim, was poured out as a means of atonement for sin.

In John 6:53-56, Jesus says that whoever drinks his blood has eternal life. Likewise, in John 7:38-39, Jesus refers to a Scripture passage: "Rivers of living water will flow from within him." John explains that Jesus was referring to the life-giving Spirit that will be given to the Church when Jesus is glorified. Thus, the blood of Jesus and the water flowing from his side are the means whereby believers share in the life of Jesus through his Spirit. Later in the Church, the blood and the water are understood to symbolize the sacraments of Eucharist and Baptism, the two principle means by which the followers of Jesus share in his life.

Questions:

16. *How does John show that Jesus fulfills the Passover sacrifice of Exodus (Exodus 12:7-10, 13, 46)?*

17. *How does John express the meaning of the blood and water in his first letter (1 John 5:6-11)?*

18. *What new understanding of Jesus' death have the passion accounts given you?*

_____

_____

_____

_____

_____

_____

_____

_____

_____

_____

_____

Lesson Five

Read Mark, chapter 16, verses 1-2

"If Christ has not been raised, then empty is our preaching; empty, too, your faith" (1 Cor 15:14). This statement of Paul captures the central importance of the resurrection of Jesus for us. Christianity is truly the faith of Easter. The death and resurrection of Jesus should not be separated from one another; they are one saving act. The earliest proclamation of the Church was that Jesus has died and is risen.

The resurrection is not just something that happened to Jesus. The early Church proclaimed that because Christ rose from the dead, we who share his life rise with him. Paul proclaimed in Romans: "We were indeed buried with him through baptism into death, so that, just as Christ was raised from the dead by the glory of the Father, we too might live in newness of life" (Rom 6:4). The resurrection transforms us here and now, not just after death, because we share in Christ's life now. Eternal life begins now as we enter into the kind of life that is worth living forever.

The letters of Paul and the Acts of the Apostles tell us a lot about what the early Church taught about resurrection. Each of the four Gospels teach about resurrection by narrating different occurrences surrounding Jesus' resurrection. They do not just report what happened, but more importantly, they express the significance of what happened. Each of them presents a different message, a different aspect of the inexhaustible mystery of the risen Lord.

The first and the shortest of these resurrection narratives was written by Mark. The resurrection account in Mark begins at sunrise, on the first day of the week. The specific emphasis on the time shows us that this event is, in fact, the beginning of a new era. The resurrection brought a fresh new beginning to the life of Jesus' followers. It was as if creation was beginning again on the first day.

Several women set out, making their way to the tomb to give the one they loved a proper preparation for burial. They were the same women who had been with Jesus along the way, as they traveled through the hills of Galilee. Not even his horrible death on the cross could undo their devotion to him. Despite their deep sorrow, they were faithful to the end.

Questions:

1. Why is the resurrection the heart of Christian faith?

2. Why did the early Church choose Sunday as the day it gathers for Eucharist?

3. In what ways do you live a new life because of the resurrection of Jesus?

_____

_____

_____

_____

_____

_____

_____

_____

_____

_____

_____

_____

_____

_____

Read Mark, chapter 16, verses 3-8

No thought of resurrection was on the minds of the women as they walked back to the site of Jesus' death and burial. The only concern they voiced was a practical one: "Who will roll back the stone for us?" The male disciples had all fled, and they were still nowhere to be found.

In a clear and concise way, Mark tells his readers the fact of the empty tomb and the reason for its emptiness. He offers no details about the resurrection, but briefly states, "He has been raised." The commission to "go and tell his disciples and Peter" does not seem to have been fulfilled. The women fled from the tomb and said nothing to anyone because of their fear and bewilderment.

The original ending of Mark's Gospel was verse 8. He refrained from describing any resurrection appearances, though he certainly knew of them and could have recounted them in his Gospel. The vocabulary and style of the longer endings indicate that they were written at a later period by someone other than Mark.

Why did Mark end his Gospel here? Mark left his Gospel open-ended because the good news of Jesus is not yet complete. It must be taken up and proclaimed anew in every generation. The women fled from the empty tomb puzzled over the meaning of the resurrection and its implication for their lives. The silence of the women expresses the reality that each individual must come to know and experience the risen presence of Jesus in their own lives.

Rather than ending his Gospel with appearances of Jesus, Mark ended with Jesus' promise. The message given to the women repeats the promise Jesus made to Peter and the disciples before his death: "After I have been raised up, I shall go before you to Galilee" (14:28). The last message of the Gospel is that Jesus has gone ahead of them and that they will see him. Jesus' first call to his disciples in Galilee, "Come after me," became the final challenge addressed to all future disciples.

Mark wanted to tell his readers that the resurrection is not the end of the story, but only a new beginning. What has begun in Jesus is still going on today. The risen Jesus continues to lead disciples as they hear his call and follow after him.

Questions:

4. *What would be your reaction if you were one of the women who discovered the empty tomb (16:8)?*

5. *Why did Mark's Gospel originally end with verse 8?*

6. *How does the fact that the tomb of Jesus was empty challenge you as a follower of Jesus today?*

_____

_____

_____

_____

_____

_____

_____

_____

_____

_____

_____

_____

Read Mark, chapter 16, verses 9-20

Since verse eight is such an abrupt ending for the Gospel, the common opinion in earlier centuries was that the ending of Mark's Gospel had been lost. So toward the end of the first century, Christians wrote other endings for the Gospel based on what they felt Mark would have written.

The longer ending contains vocabulary, themes, and a style unlike anything in Mark's Gospel. It is simply a compilation of several resurrection appearances that were commonly remembered by the early Church. The other three Gospels contain very similar accounts, but they are much more developed than those summarized here. Though written at a later period, these endings of the Gospel of Mark have always been accepted by the Church as an inspired part of the Gospel, and thus are very important for us.

Today, centuries after Mark wrote his good news about Jesus, we find ourselves deserving of the same reprimand that Jesus gave to his disciples in verse 14: "[He] rebuked them for their unbelief and hardness of heart because they had not believed those who saw him after he had been raised." Perhaps, like the disciples in the Gospel, we see our unbelief most clearly when we give in to the discouragement and frustration that comes with the challenge of following Jesus.

Yet, verse 15 is as encouraging for us as it was for the original disciples. Those who had just been reprimanded for their lack of faith were then entrusted with preaching the Gospel to the whole world. It is the risen Jesus working through his disciples who accomplishes more than we can imagine. By sharing the good news of Christ's resurrection with others, we too will be strengthened in our faith.

The proclamation of the good news of Jesus Christ, the Son of God, which began the Gospel of Mark, now concludes the work. It is up to each one of us to proclaim the Gospel as we follow Jesus. Living that good news through struggle, misunderstanding, joy, suffering, death, and resurrection is what following Jesus is all about.

Questions:

7. *Why did the disciples not believe the message that Jesus had risen?*

8. *What would your life be like if you truly believed with all your heart that Jesus is alive and risen?*

9. *What is the most important message that you want to remember from your study of the Gospel of Mark?*

_____

_____

_____

_____

_____

_____

_____

_____

_____

_____

_____

_____

_____

_____

_____

_____

Read Matthew, chapter 28, verses 1-10

Though the fact that Jesus is risen was the heart of the early Church's proclamation, details and circumstances of his appearances were not part of the earliest preaching tradition. Thus, the resurrection accounts in each of the four Gospels differ significantly. Aside from certain basic facts, each of the evangelists concluded his Gospel with resurrection accounts that express the unique message of that particular Gospel portrait of Jesus.

The end of Matthew's passion account had shown the opponents of Jesus sealing the tomb and setting a guard there. Two women had remained with Jesus at his death and stood watching the tomb at his burial. In the resurrection account the same women returned to resume their faithful vigil. Yet, the events that followed show that human power cannot frustrate God's plan. The resurrection is God's triumph over the forces of death.

What the women experienced is stunningly described only in Matthew's Gospel. First there was an earthquake which expresses the cosmic importance of what God has done in Jesus. The old world was shaking to its foundations, and the new and decisive age of salvation was beginning. By showing the earthquake both at the death of Jesus and also at his resurrection, Matthew tied the death and resurrection together into one great final event.

Next an angel of the Lord descended from heaven, rolled back the stone, and sat upon it in triumph. The human powers that sealed the tomb are as nothing when compared to the power of God shown in raising Jesus from death. The guards at the tomb "became like dead men" while Jesus was proclaimed to be alive.

The angel then gave the women a mission: "Go quickly." They were to proclaim the message of the resurrection to the disciples. Their reaction, "fearful yet overjoyed," is typical of human reaction to divine manifestations throughout the Scriptures. We, too, should show a reverential fear and a deep joy in receiving and sharing the good news of the risen Lord. As the women were privileged to be the first human proclaimers of the resurrection, we are invited by the Gospel to hear the good news and proclaim it to others.

Questions:

10. *Why are each of the resurrection accounts so different?*

11. *Why does Matthew, unlike the other Gospel writers, note the earthquake (28:2; 27:51-54)?*

12. *How is the response of the women in Matthew's account different from that in Mark (28:8; Mark 16:8)? What would be your response?*

_____

_____

_____

_____

_____

_____

_____

_____

_____

_____

_____

_____

_____

Read Matthew, chapter 28, verses 11-15

This incident of the guard's report is another event reported only by Matthew. It reflects the situation of the Church of the first century in which the opposition between Christians and Jews had become antagonism. Each sought to discredit the other and such hostility resulted in persecutions.

After narrating the appearance of Jesus, Matthew returns us to the story of the guard. The Jewish leaders who had posted the guard at the tomb (27:62-66), having failed to prevent the resurrection, tried then to render it unbelievable. Though they had heard how an angel of the Lord descended from heaven to open the tomb, they did not come to believe and continued their opposition.

In the passion account these same chief priests and elders had taken counsel on how to put an end to Jesus. They had paid Judas silver pieces to hand Jesus over and had sought false testimony to convict Jesus. Here, too, they paid silver pieces to the guards and they used falsehood to try to put an end to the resurrection story.

The last time Matthew mentioned these Jewish authorities (28:13), they were teaching the soldiers to lie about Jesus. They were told to explain the resurrection as a theft of the body by the disciples. In contrast, the last time Matthew mentioned Jesus (28:20), he was telling his disciples to teach everyone all that he had commanded them.

The story that "has circulated among the Jews to the present day" was a rumor that circulated among the people in the Church of Matthew's day. It was an attempt to refute the explanation of the empty tomb proclaimed by the Christians. Though it reflects the conditions of the early Church, it continues to demonstrate that hostility between religions does nothing to further the cause of truth. Ugly rumors and unsubstantiated reports are also characteristic of the animosity between religions today. The Gospel shows that such belligerence only harms the cause of all religions.

Questions:

13. *Why did Matthew alone include the incident about the guard at the tomb?*

14. *How do you respond to doubts about the resurrection today?*

15. *What are some examples of false and hostile rumors between religions today?*

_____

_____

_____

_____

_____

_____

_____

_____

_____

_____

_____

_____

_____

_____

_____

_____

_____

Read Matthew, chapter 28, verses 16-20

Jesus had promised the eleven disciples that they would see him in Galilee, and at the mountain Jesus fulfilled that promise. The mountain had been the place of special revelation throughout the history of salvation, from Mount Sinai to the mountain from which Jesus taught (5:1), where he went to pray (14:23), where he healed and fed the crowds (15:29), and where he was transfigured (17:1). At this mountain Jesus revealed to them his risen presence and gave them their final commission to go into all the world.

In the resurrection appearances of the various Gospels, doubt was the reaction of many. In this scene Matthew tells us that "they worshiped, but they doubted." "Doubt" here implies weakness or hesitation in faith. Such a mixture of faith and uncertainty is characteristic of discipleship. The scene reminds us that even after the resurrection, faith is not an easy response. Yet, Jesus accepted the doubting of his disciples and continued to approach them. Though they doubted, they worshiped him and received his empowerment.

Just as Jesus had carried on God's work, so the apostles received the commission to carry on Jesus' work. Because Jesus' power and authority were made universal by his death and resurrection, Jesus commissioned his disciples to a worldwide mission. The limitations of his ministry (15:24) and the restrictions he had placed on the mission of the disciples, a mission only to "the lost sheep of the house of Israel" (10:6), were overcome. The fruits of his death were to be offered to all people throughout the world, Jews and Gentiles alike.

The commissioning of the disciples reflects the threefold mission of the Church: evangelization, baptism, and teaching. The first task of the Church is the proclamation of the good news. Then new disciples are brought into the life of the Church through baptism. Finally, detailed teaching in the way of Christ must guide the new disciples.

The formula of baptism in the early Church, "in the name of the Father, and of the Son, and of the holy Spirit," reflects what it means to come into the life of God. It is the experience of Jesus' final promise, "I am with you always," through the Holy Spirit within us, leading us to unity in the family of God.

Questions:

16. *How is the response of the disciples to the risen Jesus (28:17) like or unlike your response to Jesus?*

17. *In what ways does the Church today carry out its three-fold mission to evangelize, baptize, and teach?*

18. *How does the resurrection account of Matthew give you greater hope in your desire to follow Jesus?*

Lesson Six

Read Luke, chapter 24, verses 1-12

Luke's resurrection account picks up from the sentence that concluded the burial of Jesus. The women had seen how the body of Jesus was laid in the tomb (23:55) and they went back to prepare spices and perfumed oils (23:56). After resting on the Sabbath the women went to the tomb early on the first day of the week. All the resurrection appearances of Luke's final chapter happened on this same "first day of the week." This is the first day of a new age, the day Christians had set apart each week as the day to celebrate the resurrection through the breaking of the bread (Acts 20:7).

The women found what they did not expect—the stone rolled away from the tomb; they did not find what they expected—the body of Jesus. When the two messengers appeared, they challenged the women for focusing on the tomb: "Why do you seek the living one among the dead?" This was not a time to focus on the fact that "he is not here," but on the mission implied by the fact that "he has been raised."

The experience focuses on the importance of "remembering." The women had been with the disciples in Galilee when Jesus told them that "the Son of Man must be handed over to sinners and be crucified, and rise on the third day" (24:7). When they were urged to remember what Jesus had told them, in their remembering they began to understand.

In our lives it is important to continually learn the Scriptures. Usually what we learn will not strike fire or be understood as a matter of great relevance at the time. But the times will come in our lives when we will remember and that remembering will make all the difference. Like those who experienced the risen Jesus, we will remember and then understand.

The good news that Jesus lives cannot simply be received and then kept to ourselves. It must be passed on to others and acted upon. The women were urged to leave the tomb in order to find the living one among the living. They returned to tell the good news to the eleven and all the others, but the message was not accepted because it seemed like nonsense. Only a personal experience of the risen Lord will bring the disciples to faith.

Questions:

1. *Why does Luke emphasize that the resurrection appearances happened on Sunday?*

2. *Reflect on a time when "remembering" helped you to understand an event in your life (24:6, 8)?*

3. *Why did the apostles not believe the message of the women (24:11)?*

Read Luke, chapter 24, verses 13-35

It is easy for us to envy those first disciples of Jesus who were fortunate enough to see Jesus with their own eyes. However, this account assures us that we have the same means of recognizing the presence of Jesus among us. The two disciples at Emmaus were not able to recognize the presence of Jesus until the Scriptures were explained to them and they shared the breaking of the bread with him. The Word and the Eucharist are the essential means given to us by Jesus to know him as we gather on the first day of the week. We are just as privileged as those first disciples in the opportunity to encounter the risen Jesus with faith.

Luke described the scene as a casual encounter between people making their way back home on a Sunday evening. The two travelers had been to Jerusalem for the Passover festival and another traveler overtook them from behind to share their company and conversation. Though the disciples saw him physically, they did not recognize him because they were still spiritually blind from lack of understanding.

Walking with them Jesus began to address their confusion and interpret the Scriptures for them (24:27). Only when they heard the whole message of the prophets of Israel were they able to understand God's plan for a suffering Messiah who was also glorified.

After urging Jesus to remain with them, they reclined at table together for a meal. Breaking bread was the term Luke continually used for the Eucharistic meal of the early Christians. Jesus, assuming the role of the host, gestured over the bread recalling the Last Supper. As Jesus blessed and broke the bread the disciples recognized him. "Their eyes were opened" means they understood and were able to see him with the eyes of faith.

The encounter is really about Christian worship through which Jesus truly becomes present. The ancient elements of worship—word and sacrament, Scriptures and Eucharist—are the ways that Jesus remains with us. Though the exposition of the Scriptures did not bring about recognition of Jesus, it made their hearts burn within them (24:32) and prepared them for recognition. As we allow the Scriptures to set our hearts on fire each day and as we worship on Sunday with the community of disciples, we are gradually led through understanding to recognition of the risen Lord.

Questions:

4. *When did the two disciples at Emmaus recognize Jesus (24:30-31, 35)?*

5. *How does the Emmaus account relate to our experience of worship today (24:27-35)?*

6. *When have the Scriptures caused your heart to burn within you (24:32; Heb 4:12)?*

_____

_____

_____

_____

_____

_____

_____

_____

_____

_____

_____

_____

_____

Read Luke, chapter 24, verses 36-53

The appearance of the risen Jesus provoked a variety of reactions from his disciples: they were startled, terrified, troubled, incredulous, joyful, and amazed. Jesus stood among them with his message of "peace." The greeting of peace wishes the receiver a completeness and fulfillment that is not possible to receive from the world but is experienced in the victory and risen life of Christ (1:79; 2:14; 19:42). The greeting, "Peace be with you," (24:36) became a common greeting among the early Christians expressing their new life in Christ.

This resurrection account tells us that the risen presence of Jesus was a bodily presence. In contrast to those who would interpret the resurrection as simply a return to spiritual existence, Luke insisted that Jesus' presence was a bodily reality. The disciples touched him, he showed them his hands and his feet, and he ate with them. Jesus pointed out that a ghost does not have flesh and bones as he has. Jesus convinced them that he was the same person who had lived among them before his death.

As in the Emmaus account, Luke made it clear that disciples can only understand Jesus when they understand the Scriptures. The Law, the Prophets, and the psalms is a traditional way of referring to the entire Old Testament. Interpreting these Scriptures is essential to understanding the passion and resurrection. Through the light of the resurrection it can be seen how God's plan of salvation made known in the Old Testament is fulfilled in Jesus.

The finale of Luke's Gospel is Jesus' commission of his followers to carry on the mission in his name. The disciples were to be "witnesses," beginning in Jerusalem and extending to all the nations. Jesus assured them of "power from on high," the Holy Spirit, to carry out their mission. The scene prepares for Luke's second volume, the Acts of the Apostles, which has been called the Gospel of the Holy Spirit. It begins in Jerusalem and shows how the Holy Spirit empowers the disciples to witness to Jesus "in Jerusalem . . . to the ends of the earth" (Acts 1:8).

Questions:

7. *How does Jesus' appearance to the community of disciples demonstrate that his risen presence is a bodily reality (24:39-43)?*

8. *What does the Sign of Peace mean to you during the celebration of the Eucharist?*

9. *In what ways can you be a "witness" (24:45-49)?*

_____

_____

_____

_____

_____

_____

_____

_____

_____

_____

_____

_____

_____

_____

Read John, chapter 20, verses 1-18

While all the Gospel writers began their resurrection narratives by noting that it was early Sunday morning, John alone noted that "it was still dark." Throughout his Gospel John had described discipleship as a struggle from darkness to light. In his resurrection narrative, the light began to dawn as the disciples came to believe in his risen presence.

Mary Magdalene came first to the tomb, but only long enough to see that the stone was removed and then raced off to inform the two disciples. Peter had been portrayed in other resurrection traditions as the chief witness of the resurrection. The unnamed disciple, here called "the other disciple whom Jesus loved," was introduced only in John's account. He had appeared at the Last Supper next to Jesus, in the high priest's courtyard next to Peter, and near the cross next to Jesus' mother. As a model disciple, he was shown to have the edge on Peter in both speed and insight. Though arriving at the tomb first, the other disciple did not go in, but deferred to Peter and allowed him to enter the tomb first.

The whole scene builds up to the dramatic verse: "He saw and believed." The beloved disciple believed in the risen Lord even before an appearance because of his bond of love with Jesus. Seeing the burial cloths and the wrapping left in Jesus' tomb, he knew that Jesus had been raised to eternal life.

After the two disciples returned home, Mary Magdalene was left weeping at the tomb. Unable to recognize the risen Jesus in material ways, Mary, like each of Jesus' other followers, experienced him in a new way. Mistaking Jesus for the gardener, Mary only recognized Jesus when she heard his voice, when he called her by name. John is telling us that in the spoken word of Jesus we have the means of recognizing his presence. Just as the sheep recognize the voice of the Good Shepherd when he calls their name (10:3-4), Jesus calls us personally to a relationship with him.

The beloved disciple was the first to believe; Mary Magdalene was the first to proclaim the resurrection: "I have seen the Lord." Though she wanted to hold on to Jesus, he told her that she could not experience him in the physical way she had during his earthly life. Jesus had to ascend to his Father so that a new kind of permanent relationship could begin between Jesus and his disciples through the Spirit.

Questions:

10. *In what ways is the raising of Lazarus (11:44) different from the resurrection of Jesus (20:6-7)?*

11. *Why is the beloved disciple such a model in the Gospel of John?*

12. *At what moments in your life have you felt that Jesus was truly alive and with you?*

_____

_____

_____

_____

_____

_____

_____

_____

_____

_____

_____

Read John, chapter 20, verses 19-31

Though the disciples had locked themselves from others out of fear, the presence of the risen Jesus brought them a deep sense of peace and joy. At the Last Supper Jesus had told his disciples that they would experience his gift of peace (14:27) and lasting joy (16:22) when he returned. This movement from fear to peace and joy is characteristic of the presence of the risen Jesus in the lives of all who receive his Spirit.

Jesus sent the disciples to continue his own mission: "As the Father has sent me, so I send you." What a tremendous challenge Jesus gave his followers! As the Father had sent Jesus to bring forgiveness and light and truth, so now the disciples were to carry on this same saving work. Through the power of the Spirit, Jesus would be present to the disciples, just as the Father had been present to Jesus.

As Jesus delivered forth the Holy Spirit to his disciples, he breathed on them. As God had blown his spirit or breath of life into humanity at creation (Gen 2:7), Jesus breathed his Spirit as God's people were re-created. As God's breath had made humanity in God's image, so the Spirit made the disciples into the likeness of Jesus. Just as Jesus had come to take away the sin of the world, discipleship involved the forgiveness of sins in the name of Jesus.

Thomas refused to believe the message of the disciples that Jesus had risen. He wanted a physical examination; he wanted to see with his eyes. Thomas' words, "Unless I see . . . I will not believe," expressed an attitude that had been condemned by Jesus: "Unless you people see signs and wonders, you will not believe" (4:48). Yet, when challenged by Jesus to believe, Thomas' skepticism developed into the supreme expression of Christian faith: "My Lord and my God!"

The beloved disciple, Mary Magdalene, the disciples, and Thomas had all come to believe in the risen Jesus in different ways. Now, Jesus speaks to us about the kind of belief to which we are challenged. The final praise of Jesus is for "those who have not seen and have believed." We are called to a faith that comes through hearing the Gospel, through the word of the disciples, through the invisible presence of Jesus through his Spirit. This is the kind of belief that will allow all people to come to know the blessings experienced in the risen Lord.

Questions:

13. *Why is reconciliation such an important part of the mission of discipleship (20:21-23)?*

14. *In what ways are you like Thomas (20:24-29)?*

15. *What is John's purpose in writing his Gospel (20:30-31)?*

_____

_____

_____

_____

_____

_____

_____

_____

_____

_____

_____

_____

_____

_____

Read John, chapter 21, verses 1-25

The disciples had been unsuccessful in their fishing during the night, but when Jesus came with the dawn, they brought in a huge catch. By following the directions of Jesus, they were able to do more than they could have hoped. The net full of fish symbolizes the people brought to Christ by the mission of the Church. The hundred and fifty-three fish, the number of species known at the time, represents the fullness and universality of the Church's mission.

The meal on the shore with the risen Jesus represents the Eucharist. Jesus' action with the bread and the fish echoes John's account of the Eucharistic meal eaten after the multiplication of the loaves and fish (6:11). Here the missionary disciples bring their great catch to share in the meal of communion prepared by the risen Lord. As in other resurrection accounts, the disciples recognized Jesus as they shared the meal.

While catching fish describes for John the evangelizing mission of the Church, shepherding sheep describes the pastoral mission of the Church. While Peter is the fisher-missionary, he is also the shepherd-pastor of the Church. Before Jesus assigned this role to him, Jesus asked three times, "Do you love me?" Humbled by his three-fold denial of Jesus during his passion in which Jesus had shown that he knew Peter better than he knew himself, Peter said with all his heart, "Lord, you know everything, you know that I love you."

In his three-fold command to Peter, "Feed my sheep," Jesus assigned him responsibility for the flock and commissioned him to lead the flock after his own example. In describing Peter's future death, the Gospel illustrates the sincerity of Peter's love, for Jesus said, "No one has greater love that this, to lay down one's life for one's friends" (15:13). By the time the Gospel was written Peter had already died a martyr's death, crucified like Jesus, for "a good shepherd lays down his life for his sheep" (10:11).

The disciple whom Jesus loved is shown as a model disciple throughout. He is the first to recognize the risen Christ on the shore and is shown to be the final witness as the Gospel concludes. His long life of love for Jesus is shown to be just as valid a witness as the martyrdom of Peter. The beloved disciple represents all of us as we seek to follow the risen Jesus until he comes again.

Questions:

16. *How does the great catch symbolize the life of the Church (21:1-13)?*

17. *Why does Jesus ask three times "Simon, son of John, do you love me?"*

18. *What experiences have you had that demonstrate the truth of Jesus' resurrection (21:24)*

Four Steps of Conversational Prayer*

1. *Jesus is here.*
   Realize that Jesus is with you.
   Spend a few moments in quiet, visualizing Jesus and realizing his loving presence.

2. *Thank you, Lord.*
   Express the gratitude in your heart with prayers of thanks to God.
   Mention not only the most obvious gifts of God, but especially those people and things that we may take for granted.

3. *Help me, Lord.*
   Pray for whatever you are struggling with or finding difficult about life.
   Pray for forgiveness.
   Be specific . . . be honest.

4. *Help my brother/sister.*
   Pray for others by name.
   Pray for others in the group, family members, classmates, or anyone who is in need of prayer.
   Be supportive and encouraging when others pray.

   Points to remember:
   Don't fear silence.
   Let the Holy Spirit lead you.
   Be simple, specific, and supportive.

---

*With gratitude to Rosalind Rinker, who teaches this method of personal shared prayer. See Rosalind Rinker *Learning Conversational Prayer* (The Liturgical Press, 1992).

Notes